Getting There!

It's Half the Fun

By David Messick

Original Illustrations
by Cory Steiger

Getting There!
It's Half the Fun

By David Messick
Illustrated by Cory Steiger

Text and Original Photos: David Messick
Illustrations: Cory Steiger

First Printing / Printed in the USA

ISBN: 979-8-9893939-5-4

Rainbow Puppet Publications
18 Easthill Court
Hampton, Virginia 23664
Rainbow Puppet Productions is a non-profit,
educational entertainment company

www.rainbowpuppets.com

Designed by Virginia Gabriele

Puppets included in this book were created by Laura Baldwin and
Jill Harrington

Rainbow Puppeteers include James Cooper, Wesley Huff, Alyssa Jones,
David and Joshua Messick

Thanks to
Curtis Johnson and Sentara Health Plans

Tony Gabriele, Marcy Messick, Robert Messick, Stephanie Messick,
Nancy Kent Swilley, and Rose West

To Lydia Arrington
who insisted I visit the North Carolina Transportation Museum. Her family lived in East Spencer and worked at the train shop.

That fun journey led to this book.

Contents

Foreword

When I was a kid, Sunday afternoons were almost always the same in my family. After church, my mom, dad, sister, brother, and I would pile into our little car and start driving. We often drove with no particular place in mind. That goes back to when my mom and dad were dating. They'd often hop in the car and drive around town singing away. The rest of us did the same, singing an old song like "You Are My Sunshine." My mother would sing harmony. I'd often just wish I knew where we were headed.

If we were lucky, we'd end up at my grandmother's house. If so, we were bound to enjoy her yummy fried chicken, home-made dumplings, and famous pound cake!

It was wonderful getting to my grandmother's house. Now, don't tell my family this, but it was also a lot of fun getting there.

I remembered this feeling when writing about the Wright Brothers' first trip to North Carolina to test their glider. It was quite a trip by foot, by train, and by boat. I created a song called "Half of the Fun is Getting There." So, let's start our journey... and let's have some fun along the way!

I Love Your Shoes!

Sometimes the best way to get from here to there is to walk. No fancy machines, just two feet moving. Simple and easy enough, right? Well, it can be simple and easy depending on what you are walking on. Now, if you are walking on a hot street or on a rocky mountain, you might want something to protect your bare feet.

The oldest sandals in the world were found in Fort Rock Cave in Oregon. They are about 10,000 years old. They were made out of bark and other fibers twisted together like rope.

Creative Commons, Ian Poellet

Sandals were found in many parts of the world. They provided protection from the ground below but would leave you with dirty feet.

At some point, footwear became more than just a way to protect the bottom of your feet. It could be a way to make a statement about your wealth or the type of job you had.

In Colonial Williamsburg, you can still see shoes being hand-crafted by skilled shoemakers the same way it was done almost 300 years ago. They build shoes one pair at a time. Leather is cut out. Wooden

pegs hold the heel on correctly. Then the shoe is sewn together by hand. The shoes did not lace up like many shoes do today. Instead, they were held together by a buckle. Because much travel was done by foot, soldiers of the day were issued four pairs of shoes a year.

Today, a great deal of shoe manufacturing takes place outside of the United States. Believe it or not, there is a factory in the small town of Gretna, Virginia, that still makes the dress shoes worn by every member of the Army, Navy, Marines, and Coast Guard in the United States. If you've seen a soldier in a fancy dress uniform wearing shiny black shoes, chances are they were made in Virginia.

> A factory in the small town of Gretna, Virginia, still makes dress shoes for the military.

The Capps Shoe Factory had its beginnings over 100 years ago. It started out making shoes for the government at the beginning of the 1900's. The factory was so busy making shoes for World War One and World War Two soldiers that they built dorms for their workers to live in right at the factory.

Even today, much of the work is done with custom machines and put together by hand. The

tops of the shoes are cut out using heavy metal pieces that look like a cookie cutter. These tops are stitched together by workers using sewing machines. Before the heels are added, the shoes are warmed up, one at a time, over a tiny red-hot stove. This helps flatten the bottom of the shoe. Once the heels are attached, the edges are ground to remove any rough spots. The shoes are then laced up by hand, given a super shine, and sent for final inspection.

6,000 shoes are made per week, 50 weeks a year. The whole factory takes a break at the end of December.

Athletic shoes advertised by sports heroes have exploded into a big business. Michael Jordan's fame certainly helped spring Air Jordans to worldwide popularity. They weren't the first celebrity shoes, though. That honor goes back to the 1920s when Converse All-Stars were endorsed by basketball player Chuck Taylor.

Deposit Photos

You might think the most expensive shoes on the planet are related to a sports figure. The fact is, the most expensive pair sold were worn by a movie star.

In 2024, a pair of ruby slippers from the 1939 movie "The Wizard of Oz" sold at auction for $28 million. The final price, after added fees, was $32.5 million. Those extra fees always seem to add up!

That's a lot of money for a pair of used shoes. What's more, consider this:

RadioFan at English Wikipedia

- The ruby slippers were not made out of rare ruby gemstones; they were made out of garnet-colored sequins sewn onto cloth shoes.
- These slippers weren't the only pair made for the production. There were several other pairs made. One pair is on display at the **Smithsonian** Institution in Washington, D.C. One pair is owned by a private collector. One pair is a curly-toed version that was never used in the movie.
- Back in 2005, before the auction's pair of shoes were sold, they were stolen while on display at the Judy Garland Museum in Minnesota. One of the robbers was disappointed that the shoes weren't real gemstones. He buried the shoes in a plastic case in his

Here's Tiffany Haas, "Wicked's" Glinda the Good on Broadway, holding our Dorothy puppet. Even she won't tell you what color our Dorothy's shoes are.

garden. The FBI and local police finally got the shoes returned.

- There are NO ruby slippers in the original L. Frank Baum book "The Wonderful Wizard of Oz." Instead, he wrote about magical silver slippers. The movie makers changed the shoes to ruby red because they looked better on color film.

Because of the style of puppets we use in our productions, you never see what color shoes our Dorothy puppet is wearing. Do you think they are silver, ruby, or something else? We're not telling.

Kanut Riders

Take a Horse!

Walking will only get you so far and only for so long. About five thousand years ago, people noticed that horses could run faster and longer than any human. And so began horseback riding to get from one place to another.

The earliest evidence of horseback riding is found in Europe. Four thousand years ago, horses were pulling **chariots**. That led to all sorts of wagons to transport people and goods.

Wagon wheels are often made of wood with a metal band surrounding the outside. I've been able to see this work done by **Amish** workers in Pennsylvania and by talented folks at Colonial Williamsburg.

I find the amount of math needed to create a wagon wheel to be very impressive. In the center is a hub which looks like a barrel. You have to cut notches

Cossacks, who lived near Russia and Ukraine, were not the first horseback riders but they have long been considered among the best. Our friends at Kanat Cossack Riders continue the tradition of amazing horseback riding feats.

at specific spots in the hub to insert the wooden spokes. If you don't do the math correctly, the wheel will be lopsided.

Next, you have to cut the outer rim of the wheel. Finally, a metal band is bent by hand and a blacksmith heats it up until the ends **weld** together.

The entire metal band is heated on a fire until it becomes a little larger. Because it is bigger than normal, it can be fitted onto the wooden wheel. A bucket of water is nearby in case the wood catches on fire. When the band cools, it tightens around the wheel.

Since I love the circus, I especially like to see circus wagons and wagon wheels. In order to advertise their show,

circuses would bring colorful wagons right down Main Street so people could see what would be included in the big show. You can still see many of these wagons and wagon wheels at the Ringling Museum in Sarasota, Florida.

U.S. Coast Guard

Once a year, "Saltwater Cowboys" round up wild ponies and have them swim to Chincoteague Island (chink-oh-teeg) on the Eastern Shore of Virginia. This fund raiser for the local fire department has been going on for over 100 years.

Take a Boat!

Native Americans would explore and travel the waterways in dugout canoes. They would take a log and start a fire in the center, allowing it to slowly burn a hole. They would then scrape out the insides of the log until it formed their boat.

Captains Christopher Newport and John Smith would have seen these canoes when they arrived at Jamestown in 1607. It was there that they started the first permanent English colony in America. They arrived on three boats: the Susan Constant, the Godspeed, and the Discovery. These sailing ships carried 144 men and boys and the Atlantic Ocean crossing was very difficult. Storms slowed the trip. Many passengers became sick. One died.

If you visit Jamestown today, you can see copies

Shutterstock

Shutterstock

The rough waters around Great Falls, Virginia.

The Battery Creek Lock.

of these boats and you will marvel that so many people traveled so far in such tight quarters.

During Colonial times, George Washington and others in the Virginia Colony were constantly looking for ways to move their farm goods to larger cities. Waterways were the perfect solution. Sometimes the natural waterways would be dangerous. Around Great Falls in Northern Virginia, canals were built to avoid the dangerous

Public domain

waters. You can see the remains of those canals to this day.

Near Big Island, Virginia, you can see the Battery Creek Lock. It was built in 1848 and was able to raise or lower boats 13 feet so that they could safely get their goods from higher streams onto the James River. They would then make their way to Richmond.

JolingJamesacp Wiki Commons

Goods, like tobacco and furniture, would often be transported on flat-bottom, simple boats called bateaux (bat-ohs). Once the products reached their destinations, the boats would often be sold as scrap as it would be easier to build a new one than try to get it back up river.

Today, you can ride a bateau in Scottsville, Virginia.

At the time of the Civil War, boats started to become more complex and dangerous. My great, great grandfather was actually a part of the battle of the Ironclads which was a turning point in the war. The Monitor and the Merrimac were two iron-covered

The Battle of the Monitor and the Merrimac. *Public domain*

ships that pounded each other with cannon fire. Because of their solid metal outsides, the fight ended as a draw. You can see part of the Monitor at the Mariners' Museum in Newport News, Virginia. One of our puppet makers, Laura Baldwin, helped in the restoration process after the Monitor turret was pulled up from the ocean floor.

Collis P. Huntington saw the future in building ships and so he created Newport News Shipbuilding. The first ship

The Dorothy, first boat built at Newport News Shipbuilding.

The Gerald Ford Aircraft Carrier. *US Navy*

it delivered was a tugboat called the Dorothy. The company is so proud of that boat that it has been rebuilt and can be seen today in front of the shipyard complex.

The shipyard is the largest industrial employer in Virginia. Many of my family members have worked there. My grandfather, dad, uncles, and brother worked there. I worked there one, long, hot summer and learned a lot. Today, many of my nephews work there building nuclear submarines and giant aircraft carriers.

One great memory is of my Uncle Billy. He'd spend a long day working at the shipyard only to come home to build a fishing workboat in his back yard.

Robert Messick

He’d work late into the evening. It took quite a while to make his boat and by the time it was ready, many trees had grown up in his back yard and he’d put up a big fence. Talk about being stuck. It took a little figuring to get it down to the water.

What was most fascinating was how much of the building relied on old-timers coming by to tell my uncle how to make different parts of the boat. Without their memories and help, it never would have been built.

My idea of boating involves a lot less work and is a lot more relaxing.

The Collis P. Huntington Steam Engine. *Creative Commons*

All Aboard!

There's something about a steam engine that still fascinates people of almost any age. The fable of the "Little Engine that Could" has appeared in many different versions for the last 100 or so years.

Thomas the Tank Engine is popular on television and in sold-out appearances at train museums across the country. You can ride the Hogwarts Express at a theme park in Florida. Today, there are popular fall leaf-watching train rides across the country featuring working engines of the past. Even those steam engines at theme parks like Busch Gardens and North Carolina's Tweetsie Railroad are real. They don't have a tiny electric motor hiding inside.

Steam train engines are remarkable when you think about how they work. It's like a giant tea

James Cooper holds our "Little Putt" puppet, made by Laura Baldwin.

My friend, Allison Nelson, was a train engineer at Busch Gardens, Williamsburg. She tells me you have to maintain a high level of steam to start and stop an engine. Good thing the engineer at Busch Gardens, Tampa, was paying attention when these rhinos crossed the tracks.

kettle filled with water. The water is boiled and creates steam. That steam pushes pistons, which are connected to arms that move the wheels. That's a lot of power coming from boiling water.

Trains have made a huge difference in the growth of the United States. The **Transcontinental Railroad** connected the east coast of America to the west coast. On May 10, 1869, Utah Governor Leland Stanford drove a golden stake into the ground marking the completion of a difficult construction project. Collis P. Huntington was part of that ceremony. I suspect his brain was already thinking up ways to connect trains and boats to make American products

Public Domain

available to the world.

Imagine what was necessary for this long train track to be built from Iowa to San Franciso. The builders had to make sure there was a water and fuel supply to power the engines. Cities and towns would compete to be along the train line, because that meant they could sell their goods and receive supplies easily.

In addition, builders must consider inclines like hills and mountains. Steam engines can only climb upward a small amount, so steep mountains and hills are out of the question. Trains can either travel very long distances around mountains or travel through them.

The Blue Ridge Tunnel was dug through the Afton Mountain in Central Virginia. French engineer Claudius Crozet (Crow-zay) determined that a tunnel almost one mile long could be built to handle train traffic. This was in the days before dynamite could more easily blow through the rock. Instead, the job was done with black gun powder explosions and picks, hammers, and shovels.

The work was accomplished by 800 Irish workers and 40 enslaved people of African descent. During the construction, 189 people died, most of them from a disease called **cholera** (caller-ah). Because of the dangers of the work, the enslaved people were forbidden to actually go inside the tunnel as it was constructed. They provided support work outside.

The tunnel was completed in 1858, eight years after it was started and five years past the planned date.

The tunnel saw great use until 1944. Too small to handle modern trains, its replacement was built beside the original. Today, the tunnel is a park. You can walk the almost one-mile trail. You'll want to take a good flashlight because it gets very dark. You'll also want to take a good hat because it drips lots of water from the ceiling and down the side walls.

Given the difficulty and dangers of carving

Historic Postcard

out a tunnel through rock, imagine the joy railroaders felt in finding a tunnel already carved through a mountain. The Natural Tunnel in Scott County, Virginia, was created by a stream slowly working its way through a tall mountain. In 1894, it was transformed into a railroad tunnel that is still in use today. You can take a chairlift down the mountain to see the opening. It's part of Natural Tunnel State Park.

The 611 J-Class Steam Engine is still in operation.

Public domain screen images.

A train resembling the powerful J-Class trains built in Roanoke, Virginia, appeared in a 1942 Superman cartoon. According to the animated film, the only thing more powerful than this steam engine was Superman himself.

This beautiful carousel was once at Buckroe Amusement Park. People would take a trolley all the way to the park just to ride these horses. You can still ride them, right outside of the Virginia Air and Space Science Center in Hampton, Virginia.

"To the End of the Line!"

Train tracks weren't just used to guide long trains across the country. In the days before people owned their own vehicles, they needed a way to get from their homes to work or to downtown shopping areas. Many cities put train tracks right down their streets and operated a trolley system.

The earliest trolley systems were powered by horses. Other systems, called cable cars, had a continuous steel wire cable that ran the length of the route. This steam-powered cable pulled the cars around town. Later, electric wires were hung above the tracks which then powered the cars.

Ocean View Station Museum

Trolley owners soon noticed that ridership went way down on the weekend. That's when amusement parks showed up, usually on the outskirts of town or near beaches in coastal towns. People would take the trolley to the end of the line to meet friends and ride carousels, Ferris wheels, and thrilling wooden roller

Jim Wilson / Kathy Dermanis

coasters.

Those old roller coasters with wooden tracks may have looked like they would fall over at any moment, but they were quite secure. When Ocean View Amusement park closed in Norfolk, a movie crew came to record the old roller coaster falling down. For two days they used explosives to try to bring it down.

Boston Public Library cc 2.0

Above, Ocean View at quieter times.
Left, Photo illustration of the author at the Ocean View Station Museum sitting in a Rocket Roller Coaster car that survived the explosion.

In the end, they had to saw off wooden beams holding it up and use strong bulldozers to pull the coaster down!

While the coaster didn't survive, you can still have a seat in one of the original coaster cars, preserved at the Ocean View Station Museum.

Trolleys have disappeared from most cities across the country, but you can ride them in places like New Orleans, Louisiana, and Toronto, Canada. The cable car in San Francisco will still take you up and down the many hills of that city. It is interesting that in places like Norfolk, Virginia, light rail has made a comeback. The train tracks and electric wires look a lot like the old trolley systems.

Left, a New Orleans trolley car and right, a San Francisco cable car. Both are still in operation. *Shutterstock*

SCHOOL BUS
17

CAUTION

Take a Bus!

Buses, which offer more flexibility to change routes, eventually took over public transportation in most American cities.

According to the National School Transportation Association, school-aged children take over 50 million bus trips a day. That's a lot of folks on a lot of buses. Maybe you rode on a school bus today.

School-aged children take over 50 million bus trips a day.

BusWhere? tells us that the first motorized bus appeared in 1914. Before that time, horse-drawn wagons were used.

Buses were not officially painted "School Bus Yellow" until 1939. That was to help them be more visible on the road.

Take a look at this bus in the Virginia Transportation Museum. It has benches for seats and the walls are made of wood, not metal. It sure looks different from what schools use today.

COBRA

"I Get Around!"

In the "land of the free," Americans love the ability to take a car wherever they want without being tied down to train tracks and trolley lines, without being stuck on specific bus routes.

While Henry Ford didn't invent the gasoline-powered automobile, his way of making them on an assembly line made the car affordable for many Americans. Instead of a team of workers building a car from the ground up, one at a time, he had a different vision. Workers would specialize in one of many parts of the process. One team would install the motor. Another team added the wheels. Another team would add the bumper. The cars would follow a track throughout the warehouse and deliver one car after another.

The work could be boring as workers would do the same task over and over throughout the day. Henry realized this and so he raised their pay to make the job more appealing.

Shutterstock

Public Domain

In addition, with higher wages, his workers could then afford the product they made. To compete for workers, nearby companies would raise their wages as well, creating more buyers of Henry Ford's Model T automobile.

Henry Ford once said, "Any customer can have a car painted any color that he wants so long as it is black." The truth is, several other colors were also available including green, grey, and red.

From the moment the first Model T rolled out of the shop in 1908 until today, people have loved their cars. In the 1960s movies celebrated fast cars and the Beach Boys sang many hit songs about their favorites including their first number one hit, "I Get Around."

Cars come in all shapes and sizes. This one resembles a bottle for holding hot coffee.

If you think electric cars are a new thing, think again. The Detroit Electric Car was built in 1913!

The longest automobile to date is the American Dream Limousine. It's in the **Guinness** Book of World Records and is 100 feet from end to end.

Almay

With so many cars requiring so much gasoline, many car makers looked for ways to improve gas consumption. One way was to create better engines. Another would be to make smaller cars.

The smallest mass-produced automobile is the Peel P50. Created in 1962, it has only three wheels and room for one passenger and a shopping bag. It was built in England. Now it is mostly seen at car shows and in museums.

If you think Peel P50 is difficult to squeeze into, wait until you see Lou Jacobs' circus car. Lou is one of the most famous clowns in history and one of his most famous acts was driving a tiny car into the circus arena. He would then plop out his giant clown feet and slowly curl out of the vehicle. With his tall fake

forehead and circus hat, he'd reach over six feet tall. It was quite a sight to see this huge clown slide out of his little car.

To be clear, his car really drove. It was powered by a washing machine motor! You can see it today at the Ringling Circus Museum in Sarasota, Florida. They even have a full-sized model that you can try to get into. Even if you can squeeze into his car, remember that you also have to get out!

LMS DCC / Creative Commons

The US Postal Service has a rule that no living person is to be featured on a postage stamp. That has held true to this day with one exception. In 1966, Lou Jacobs, in full clown face, was featured on a US Postage Stamp.

An average car today is pretty easy to start. Imagine taking a half hour to start an engine.

Shutterstock

Back in the 1920s there was a rise in the use of bulb engine vehicles for farms and other locations. These vehicles would be run on easy to obtain crude oils and kerosene. They did not need gasoline, which became more and more difficult to obtain because of war usage around the world.

These vehicles were usually slow moving and very slow to start. Here's how it worked. First, you'd take

a blowtorch (Yes! A real blowtorch!) and heat up a large metal bulb on the front of the vehicle. This usually took about 20 to 30 minutes. Once the bulb became red hot, you would take the steering wheel off its usual location and put in on the side of the vehicle where you'd spin it around to start the motor. If the bulb was hot enough, the engine would start. If not, it was back to heating the bulb and spinning the wheel again.

Because of the effort, most children on the farm would prefer to collect eggs or milk the cows rather than have engine-starting duty. Once the engine was started, farmers would usually keep it running all day to avoid the starting process again.

I'm so grateful that my car starts with a push of a button!

Ride a Bike

The bicycle industry reports that over 20 million bicycles are sold in the United States every year. Five million of those sales happen in December when many lucky children find a bike under the Christmas tree.

As popular as bikes are today, it's hard to understand what a difference they made to people one hundred years ago. While cars are a great way to get around, they were too expensive for many working people. The safety bicycle, with two equal-sized wheels and driven by a chain, made personal transportation available to many people.

Imagine being a factory worker stuck in the big city all week. A bicycle opened up new places to visit and explore.

This style of bike was invented in the 1880s. They weren't called a "safety bicycle" for nothing. Before they were created, there were bicycles with a giant front wheel and a small back wheel. The front wheel was moved by foot power

A Wright Brothers safety bike. *Wiki Commons*

without the help of a chain and gear to increase the power. If you didn't maintain your balance, there was quite a fall. If you weren't in great shape, you'd tire out quickly.

Public Domain

Today, BMX stunt bikes and amazing riders challenge the idea of "safety bikes." They bring a sense of excitement and possible danger to the world of bikes. Just ask my mother. She'll tell you of the time my brother built a giant ramp and rode bikes off the roof of our house! I don't think you should try this at your home.

Shutterstock

THE WRIGHT

We Can Fly!

Believe it or not, the safety bicycle helped lead the way to one of the greatest inventions of the last century, the flying machine.

Orville and Wilbur Wright, two bike-building brothers from Dayton, Ohio, learned many lessons while making bicycles in their shop. They learned about gears and chain drives. They learned about the importance of safe and proper steering. They also spent their free time reading about all the amazing people around the world racing to create their own flying machine. At some point, Orville and Wilbur went from reading to dreaming and finally building their own flying machine.

At some point, Orville and Wilbur went from reading to dreaming and finally building their own flying machine.

On December 17, 1903, on the sandy Outer Banks of North Carolina, they flew the first self-propelled airplane. It started a revolution of flight that continues to this day.

Believe it or not, the first airplane was steered by the pilot lying on his stomach and moving his hips back and forth!

It didn't take long to determine there had to be a better way to steer. A hand operated steering mechanism is in this plane, made famous by the Tuskegee Airmen.

Creative Commons

Creative Commons

The first flight of an airplane lasted only 12 seconds and traveled only 120 feet. Today, the Airbus A350-900 URL (Ultra Long Range) can stay in the air for up to 20 hours and travel 9,700 miles.

Below, our team celebrates the work of the Wright Brothers. They solved three problems in order to fly: Power, Lift, and Control.

U.S. Army Transportation Museum Fort Eustis, VA

Can That Thing Fly?

Like many kids growing up, I loved science fiction movies and television shows. They were a big deal when I was young. They still are today. But my friends and I were especially lucky. We could say we had a real-life flying saucer in our town. And we really did.

I grew up in Newport News, Virginia. It's the home of Fort Eustis which, at the time, was the home of the US Army Transportation Corps. As you would drive on post, you would go by a real-life flying saucer! It was one of many amazing transportation experiments by the army.

My dad and I would visit their Transportation Museum from time to time. Once we even got to ride

Shutterstock

U.S. Army Transportation Museum Fort Eustis, VA

a train around the post. It was the first time either of us had been on a train.

Still, it was the flying saucer that always caught my eye. It was one of many experiments to find ways to move people and equipment. You can only see a few parts of the flying saucer today. It seems that they took the machine apart for cleaning and maintenance and now can't seem to put it back together!

Another unusual vehicle was an HZ-1 Aero cycle which looks a bit like a pogo stick with a helicopter blade at the bottom. One slip on that machine could be deadly. As they soon learned, the blades would flex at certain speeds and come down with a crash.

And there was more. Maybe you remember the

Shutterstock

U.S. Army Transportation Museum Fort Eustis, VA

AT-AT Walker (All Terrain Armored Transport) from the Star Wars movies? The army experimented with that idea way before the film came out.

They also had cars that could hover over land and water. Quite a sight to see.

Finally, perhaps you've seen action heroes like James Bond zip into the sky with a jet pack on their back? The army experimented with that as well and had public demonstrations to prove it.

I wondered why all of these strange machines were built, and Joseph Scanlin, the Director of the Fort Eustis Transportation Museum, told me it was to find new ways to move people and equipment. In the end, the helicopter proved the best choice for many jobs. They are more reliable and need less repair service.

Creative Commons 3.0

There is one unusual flying machine that has proven to be very successful. Many, many years ago, we were performing on a field at Fort Eustis as part of their Super Day family event. All of a sudden, the thousands of guests froze in their tracks as the Stealth Bomber flew overhead. Most people had never heard of or seen this thing before. Now it was flying so close it seemed like we could touch it. To me, it looked like something out of a Batman movie.

U.S. Army Transportation Museum Fort Eustis, VA

Other flying vehicles are part of the collection at Fort Eustis.

To the Moon and Beyond!

I remember a day in 1969 when my family was driving home from my grandmother's house. If you started this book at the beginning, yes, I suspect we had great fried chicken and dumplings while we were there. Our path took us past the NASA Langley Research Center in Hampton, Virginia. We were soon aware of a strange glow coming through the woods. In the distance we saw a flashing light rise and lower. At first it looked like something out of a space movie. We heard a loud sound that, to me, resembled a broken vacuum cleaner. We pulled our car over next to the nearby swamp, and through the fog, we continued to see the blinking light rise and lower.

NASA

It was our astronauts practicing for a moon landing on the Lunar Excursion Module Simulator.

Many decades later a NASA employee told me that Neil Armstrong was laser focused on making the landing perfect and practiced long after others felt he had done enough. It's a good thing he understood when things weren't right. In later practice exercises in Texas, his test vehicle went out of control and he had to parachute to safety as the test module crashed and burned.

NASA

The team went back to the drawing board, made corrections, and Neil practiced even more.

It's also a good thing he practiced so much. As he was landing the real Lunar Module on the moon, computer alarms went off and he had to use the manual controls to land safely.

The entire world held their breath as he finally stepped out of the module and put his footsteps on the moon. He said at the time, "That's one small step for man. One giant leap for mankind."

Our space program continues to make advances. There are now plans to take us to Mars.

At one time, only highly trained astronauts had the opportunity to travel into space. Now, with enough money, almost anyone can take a trip into space thanks to companies like Blue Origin and Elon Musk's SpaceX.

NASA

NASA

Final Words

Well, we've made it to the end of our journey. As you can see, there are so many ways to get from here to there. So now I ask you, if you could go anywhere, where would you go? How would you get there?

No matter what you choose, enjoy the journey along the way.

Thanks

Thanks to the following people and organizations that helped make this book possible. In every case, these fine people dropped everything that they were doing to help me learn something new:

Kathy Gasparis-Dermanis of the Buckroe Improvement League in Hampton, Virginia.

Charlie Fleetwood and John Murray of the Ocean View Station Museum in Norfolk, Virginia.

Mendy Flynn and John Jamison of the Virginia Museum of Transportation in Roanoke, Virginia.

John Glover and the staff of the Capp Shoe Corporation in Gretna, Virginia.

Joseph "Sepp" Scanlin, Director of the US Army Transportation Museum at Fort Eustis, Virginia.

Dylan Simmons of the Keystone Antique Truck and Tractor Museum in Colonial Heights, Virginia.

Broadus, Joseph, Valentine, and Victoria of the Colonial Williamsburg Foundation.

Vocabulary

Amish – a religious group who avoid many modern conveniences. They still use horse and buggies to get from place to place.

chariot – a two-wheeled wagon pulled by horses.

cholera – a disease often caused by unsafe food or water.

Guinness Book of World Records, a listing of great achievements.

Smithsonian Institution – a collection of great museums in the Washington, DC area.

Transcontinental Railroad – A railroad line from California to Iowa that connected to trains that made it to the East Coast of the United States.

weld – to join pieces of metal together by applying red-hot heat.

Which of our books have you read?

Books written by David Messick and
illustrated by Liu Light and Cory Steiger

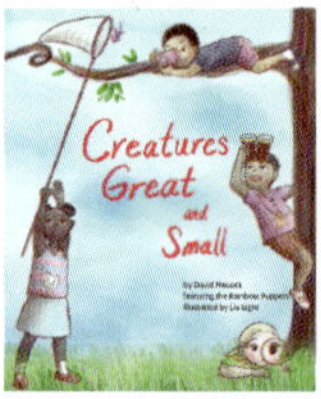

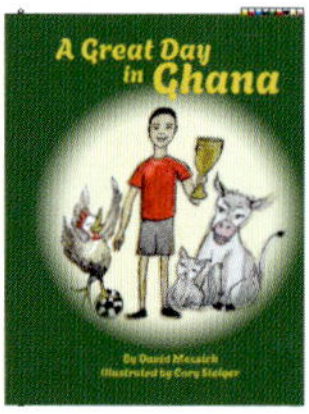

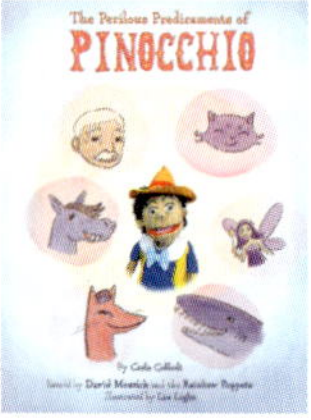

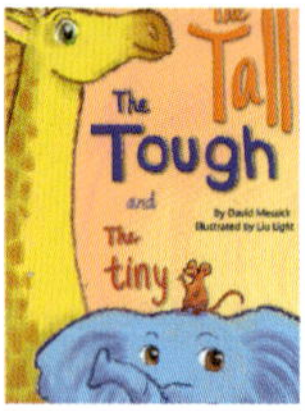

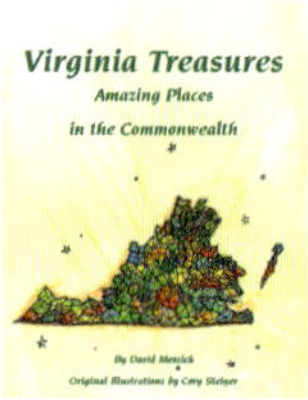

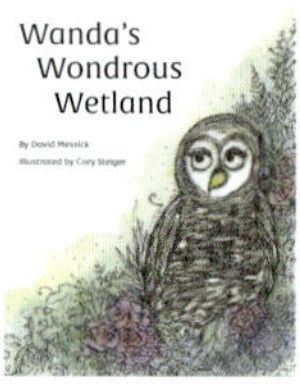